What Others Say About Alicia and Her ALIGN Process

"Alicia is a master at mindset work. As a multi-seven-figure business owner, I know that this type of work is the biggest differentiator between success and failure. If I had to pick just one thing to focus on as a person and an entrepreneur, it would be mindset and energy."

Margy Feldhuhn
CEO, Interview Connections
InterviewConnections.com l Margywithahardg.com

"Alicia is the greatest gift in my life! In just the first eight months working with her, I experienced huge transformation in both my professional and personal life! I went from two to three clients a week, to back-to-back clients paying double my original rate! I went from a two-bedroom rental apartment to buying my own home and property in a gorgeous neighborhood!

"Above all, I finally discovered what real self-empowerment is, and that is a game changer! With Alicia I have created a better life for myself and my family!

"I am forever grateful!"

Esther Stark – ACC

"Alicia Cramer is one wise, gifted soul. As her client, I feel blessed to be the beneficiary of her vast knowledge, intelligence, and guidance. In this book, you will find answers to life's most profound questions, as well as an understanding of how our vibration dictates our reality, thus regaining our power to co-create. With her no-nonsense approach, Alicia takes a deep concept and creates a simple masterpiece."

R.K.

"Alicia has helped me grow in every area of life and business by leaps and bounds. I especially gained a newfound level of empowerment in working together with her. Alicia's presence in it of itself is so empowering and valuable. Her work is truly magical. I used to get stuck in negative emotions for long periods of time, and she showed me how I can authentically release them and raise my vibrations so easily and quickly. Her clean and high-level belief in her clients makes her a priceless gift!"

C.S.

"Since I started to do work with Alicia, my life has expanded in all areas! My business especially is continuing to grow quickly and beyond my expectations! Alicia is wise, loving and cares deeply. She has a powerful way with people that inspires them to rise above their perceived limitations! If you are ready to take your life to the next level, sign up with Alicia."

D.S.

Energetic Alignment

The Power to Create a Life of Confidence, Success, and Purpose

By Alicia Cramer, C.Ht., M.Msc.

Energetic Alignment
The Power to Create a Life of Confidence, Success, and Purpose

Published by Conscious Marketing Strategies

Direct correspondence to:
AC Intl LLC
12112 N Rancho Vistoso Blvd
Ste 150 #444
Oro Valley, AZ 85755

Copyright © 2022 AC Intl LLC
All rights reserved. No part of this book may be reproduced, stored in a retrieval system, or transmitted in any form or by any means without the written permission of the publisher, except as permitted by U.S. copyright law.

ISBN: 979-8-3732757-8-1

Cover design by JS Graphic Design

DISCLAIMER AND/OR LEGAL NOTICES

While the publisher and author have used their best efforts in preparing this book, they make no representations or warranties with respect to the accuracy or completeness of the contents of this book. The advice and strategies contained herein may not be suitable for your situation. You should consult a professional where appropriate. Neither the publisher nor the author shall be liable for any loss of profit or any other commercial damages, including but not limited to special, incidental, consequential, or other damages. The purchaser or reader of this publication assumes responsibility for the use of these materials and information. Adherence to all applicable laws and regulations, both advertising and all other aspects of doing business in the United States or any other jurisdiction, is the sole responsibility of the purchaser or reader.

This book is intended to provide accurate information with regard to the subject matter covered. However, the author and the publisher accept no responsibility for inaccuracies or omissions, and the author and publisher specifically disclaim any liability, loss, or risk, whether personal, financial, or otherwise, that is incurred as a consequence, directly or indirectly, from the use and/or application of any of the contents of this book.

Dedication

For Eden and Oriana, the two best things that ever happened to me. You both have inspired me to be the best I can be, to love fully, give abundantly, appreciate daily, be a positive influence, and have a positive impact. My desire for you is to love yourself no matter what, follow your heart no matter what, and be a source of light wherever you go. Love, mom.

To the Reader

I also want to make this dedication section to you, the one reading this book. If you've felt like the outcast, felt misunderstood, questioned how and why there could possibly be so much darkness in the world when you know in your heart that life should be good... then you are in good company. It is the slightly weird ones that make positive waves that change the world for the better. Continue to be the truth seeker. Know in your heart with absolute certainty that you not only deserve goodness, but you are ultimately the creator of it.

It has been said that the material world we are living is a shadow world. That what we experience is a shadow of our previous thoughts, beliefs, expectations and imaginings. Choose what you will create in the mind now, so that you can enjoy the evidence of it later.

Table of Contents

Foreword 3
Preface 5
Everything Is Energy 7
Awareness 13
Learn 25
Identify 39
Gain Momentum 49
Nexus Point 61
What to Do Now! 69
Introduction to the Emotional Vibrational Scale 71
Introduction to Emotional Freedom Techniques (EFT) 77
Introduction to Self-Hypnosis 79
Resources: 84
About the Author 88

Foreword

Energetic Alignment is far more than a self-help book full of platitudes and feel good "you can do it" quotes. What Alicia Cramer has written, and specifically what she openly shares about her ALIGN process, is essentially a roadmap with actionable steps on how to achieve higher levels of success.

As an author and small business coach, I am frequently asked to review and recommend books by other entrepreneurs. As much as it is an honor to be asked, I have to say no to most requests purely based on my busy schedule.

When my friend and client, Alicia Cramer, asked me if I would consider writing the foreword to her new book, I will confess that it was an easy yes! Before I tell you why, let me share one of my favorite quotes from Audrey Hepburn.

"Nothing is impossible. The word itself says 'I'm Possible!'"

This simple quote is often attributed to the benefits of having a positive attitude. However, to me it says much more about the power of a healthy mindset, free of limiting thoughts and fear-based beliefs.

As Alicia so eloquently writes, "Energetic Alignment is our most powerful state. Our most fulfilled state. Our most divine state. It is when our mind, our emotions, and our spiritual self are all congruent. That's when life seems magical, as though the universe supports us in virtually everything we do."

I am a serial entrepreneur turned business coach who early on suffered from fear and limiting thoughts. I tried many things along the typical "self-help" routes, but it wasn't until I worked with a hypnotherapist that the growth of my businesses, and ultimately my happiness, really took hold.

Foreword

What Alicia has done by creating her ALIGN process, is describe upfront, to potential clients and the readers of this book, what is possible, and how she is able to help so many people. I find this approach very refreshing as many people who do this type of work do not like to "show their cards" before working with someone.

I could go on about this book and Alicia Cramer; clearly I am a big fan. But let me leave you with this: If you'd like to achieve more in your career or business, if you desire to have a life that you truly love, I encourage you to read this book and, if possible, connect with Alicia Cramer, and discover the power to create a life of confidence, success, and purpose. Yes, it is possible.

I'll close with this quote from Napoleon Hill, author of *Think and Grow Rich*: "Keep your mind fixed on what you want in life; not on what you don't want."

Cap't Jim Palmer – The Dream Business Coach
www.GetJimPalmer.com

Preface

Before we get started, I am going to take this opportunity to share something important: This book is incomplete. Like any true and enlightened quote that evokes inspiration, there are nuances that have not been articulated and expanded upon. Like every beautiful ah-ha you have, there is more depth yet to be discovered. And within this book, we really just scratch the surface of deeper concepts.

That being said, there are so many valuable principles for you inside this book. You can learn by applying each concept at your current level, and as you revisit the concept later, you can learn yet again at an even deeper level. Like all personal growth, you can pursue it as shallow or deep as you choose. There is so much knowledge available to you from a wide variety of sources, and this book, while certainly advanced in many ways, is just the beginning.

I also want to make a disclaimer. I have two motives for this book. One is my deeper mission and calling, which is to empower others through higher truth. The other is to bring you further into my world where I can help you at a much deeper level. You will see many calls to action about my Business Mastery Academy throughout this book. And I am not going to apologize for that because I know that I can help you far beyond what we cover in the chapters to follow. You do not need to join the Academy to benefit from this information, just know that more support is available to you if you want it.

With all of that said, I sincerely thank you for choosing to go on this journey with me; I am so grateful to play a small part on your path to greater success and empowerment.

Preface

Introduction
Everything Is Energy

Originally, I was going to title my next book, "F@ck Limiting Beliefs." A few friends and colleagues thought it was a great idea, and a couple people were not so sure. After all, it's those limiting beliefs (what I sometimes refer to as "Mental F*kery") that not only slow you down but can keep you stuck. But after tuning into the real essence of what I want to empower my readers with, I opted for the current title, *Energetic Alignment*, which is really the core of what I mentor my clients toward and what I help them achieve as we work together.

Energetic Alignment is our most powerful state. Our most fulfilled state. Our most divine state. It is when our mind, our emotions, and our spiritual self are all congruent. That's when life seems magical, as though the universe supports us in virtually everything we do.

A client I'll call "CT" first came to me with many years of experience in business online. He had some really big wins and some really big losses. He was still traumatized by the losses, and although he didn't use that word specifically, he knew that left unaddressed, his past failures would continue to adversely affect his success mindset and hinder the future growth of his business. He was experiencing some financial challenges when we started working together, and the stress was taking its toll. Working together, we identified many of his limiting and fear-based beliefs. CT had been struggling with a lot of insecurities which were affecting his confidence and found himself frequently comparing himself to his colleagues. We had to clean up his mindset (including his money mindset) and get him into a state of energetic alignment with his goals.

Of course, our state of alignment is not a fixed state. We encounter old emotionally charged triggers, get caught up in the dramas of life, and sometimes veer off course in pursuit of other people's ideas of success and fulfillment. Yet, despite a lifetime's worth of less-than-empowering mental conditioning, limiting beliefs, and not-so-great habits, we can get into our state of alignment and experience incredible blessings, abundance, success, and fulfillment.

In CT's case, after working together for four short months, he not only gained greater alignment and shifted his mindset, going from feelings of disempowerment, stress, and low self-esteem to feeling more confident, his business began growing again. In addition to the mental and emotional breakthroughs, he was able to manifest circumstances in his life that put over $1 million in his bank account. He went from massive debt and the stress that goes with that to cleaning up his energy and mindset to get his business and life back on track.

In another example of the power of the ALIGN process, "AB" first came to me wanting help with smoking cessation when I had my general hypnotherapy practice. After he successfully quit smoking, he decided to continue our work together and became a long-term client. When we started, he was working in the family business, a distribution company, which he didn't love. He was an aspiring serial entrepreneur who wanted to create his own wealth and do his own thing. After several months of working together, he was able to exit the family business, with a $20+ million purchase price, and went on to pursue other businesses in the food industry and in real estate investments.

I like both examples because they demonstrate that regardless of your industry, your goals, your current mental and emotional state, or your existing circumstances… you can create awesome things in your life and business.

The Process

This book is based on my ALIGN process, which is the process I take all my clients through regardless of whether they are on the fast track, working with me intensely, or they take the slower route, working with me less frequently.

Here are the steps in the ALIGN process:

AWARENESS: The beginning of your life-changing transformation starts with first becoming aware of the old patterns and long-held mental programs that are keeping you stuck and on a recurring loop, repeating behaviors that result in failure to achieve what you want.

LEARN: Throughout the early stages of the ALIGN process, you will learn the processes to experience life-shifting transformation and begin to master your mind and emotions. This is a skill like any other, and it takes understanding and practice.

IDENTIFY: At this third stage of the ALIGN process, together we'll reveal your true desires and begin to move forward into alignment with your higher calling, armed with new confidence and purpose.

GAIN MOMENTUM: Throughout this ALIGN process, you'll experience consistent breakthroughs, some small and some groundbreaking – but all will manifest positive changes in your life.

NEXUS POINT: This inner transformation process launches you into the realization of your biggest goals and desired outcomes – creating a life and business you love – experiencing **energetic alignment**! Success in life and in business is the next natural step when you've aligned your mind with your heart's desires. True alignment is where confidence, success, and purpose originate and thrive.

I've written this book to be more of a manual for transformation and getting into your state of alignment, than the conventional self-help book designed to motivate or inspire you. We'll look at the broader concepts and then dive into the details in each chapter as we cover each part of the process. That said, you are encouraged to read, then re-read this book, allowing yourself time to process what you've read, apply it, and see evidence of it working in your life.

My Story

So, you want to overcome your limiting beliefs and achieve the alignment I've described, but you may be wondering why you should listen to me about this topic. I'd say I've been where you are, but it's possible that I was even worse off than you are now.

Around age 12, I became severely depressed, living in a toxic environment, to the point of resorting to alcohol to self-medicate and battle suicidal feelings that followed me into adulthood. I didn't have positive influences and bounced back and forth from anger to depression. The emotional pain I was experiencing was very real. I was extremely self-conscious, self-destructive, and had very low self-esteem. If anyone would have suggested I'd be where I am today, I would have told them they were out of their mind.

Yet, here I am today – a highly respected mindset expert, coach, and certified hypnotherapist who's an author, public speaker, have been interviewed on numerous shows and in articles, and served as an expert panelist on TV. How does someone who struggled with alcoholism, major depression, and significant self-esteem issues break free to achieve inner alignment and the confidence and success that follow? In 2005, I was assaulted, and it was a terrifying and emotionally devasting experience. However, it became a catalyst. I had two options: let the fear and trauma kill me or find a cure. I chose the latter.

My commitment to find relief from the pain led me to hypnotherapy, EFT, and energy healing. The results were so profound, I made it my life's work to learn, refine, and implement these and other modalities in the ALIGN process that I now use to help my clients. Plus, I have an extensive background in both marketing and business development, which helps me really understand other entrepreneurs and their mindset challenges. When it comes to entrepreneurship, I can honestly say, "Been there, done that," including struggling with my first online business to the point of bankruptcy, and plenty of ups and downs while experiencing life in the trenches in my other businesses. At the time of this book, I've been helping clients for well over a decade and have an international client and customer base.

In addition to more practical skills, I began to embrace and utilize my natural intuitive capabilities to identify my clients' subconscious and energetic blocks, enabling me to help shift them quickly using a variety of techniques that I have become highly proficient at over the years.

So you see, I truly understand what you're facing and why you picked up this book in the first place.

For now, let's get to it... your true self is calling for you to step up and create a life and business that you love, and I'm excited to begin the journey with you..

Everything Is Energy

Chapter One

Awareness

Awareness is multi-faceted because it means a few different things and goes beyond the dictionary definition: "knowledge and understanding that something is happening or exists."

The first awareness that I want to cover is what I call foundational awareness. It's an understanding of how the universe works and how your mind works. One of the places where we need to start is to gain a solid understanding of the law of vibration. We really do live in a law-based universe. Most people accept that the law of gravity is, in fact, a law and applies to everyone, regardless of their beliefs. The law of vibration is something we understand from physics. We know (and learned from Einstein) that everything is energy, and people understand this on a high level. However, a lot of people fail to understand just how fundamental this principle is with respect to creating a life that is fulfilling... a life that is, essentially, the life we want to live. We are designed to be empowered, deliberate creators in our lives, not simply reactors to circumstances – feeling disempowered and bumping through life feeling out of control and unfulfilled.

When I'm referring to the law of vibration, you need to remember that *everything has its own vibrational frequency*, including our thoughts and including our emotions. You may have heard about the law of attraction (perhaps from the movie, *The Secret*) and references to manifesting your goals, dreams, and desires. Many coaches preach the law of attraction, and you've probably scrolled through your social media feed and seen plenty of fluffy quotes about this particular law. However, most people get tripped up because they don't have the full understanding of what the law of attraction really is. They're missing key elements in their understanding. If you took the individual who's trying to manifest their dream business who knows they want the money, the better lifestyle, and more clients, but in their attempt to "manifest" using the law of attraction – with vision boards, positive affirmations, and other attempts to be a vibrational match to what they want – they don't realize that their own emotions act as an indicator of whether or not they're actually in alignment with what it is they want.

Feelings as Indicators

This brings us to the second piece of awareness: understanding that our feelings will be indicators as to what we're actually thinking and vibrating and whether we're congruent with our desires or incongruent with them. Feelings are something that most people try to avoid. They'd rather never feel sad or angry as though there is something inherently wrong with those emotions. They don't realize there is a vibrational spectrum, and our emotions are our interpretation of where we are with respect to various subjects.

> *There is nothing wrong with experiencing negative emotions; they indicate when we're defaulting to limiting beliefs.*

Most people can relate to a feeling of heaviness or of feeling constricted or contracted when they're feeling a lower vibrational emotion, like sadness, depression, or even anger. And most can relate to a feeling of a higher vibrational emotion, like the expansive feeling of love or the light feeling of joy. Our emotions are not only indicators of the vibration in which we find ourselves, they're also indicators of when we're defaulting to an old limiting belief.

The term "limiting belief" essentially is: "I believe something that is not serving me or is not helping me to achieve my desired state or my desired goal or outcome." The belief, in and of itself, is preventing you from what you want. When we experience one of our limiting beliefs, we can feel the physical sensation of that misalignment as heaviness or contraction. We also experience it as an emotion – some sort of negative emotion. Virtually anyone will say, "It doesn't feel good when…." We understand that they are referring to a negative emotion associated with what they are experiencing.

If your goal is to lose 20 pounds and when you think about that goal, you notice that you feel bad, the cause of that negative feeling is that limiting beliefs are triggered. If you would be aware of that sensation as an indicator, now you could clean up those limiting beliefs that are creating resistance and roadblocks on your path to achieving your goal. That feeling is letting you know that something is off in your thinking and in your beliefs. If we were to dissect that and really challenge what's going on in your mind, you're going to notice, for example, a belief like, "No matter what I try, I always revert back to my same old bad habits. I'm never going to achieve my ideal weight." That thought happens so quickly because it's programmed deep inside your subconscious mind, and under most circumstances, the average person will not be aware enough to acknowledge that the limiting belief exists, nor will they have the awareness that there is something they can do to actually clean it up and liberate themselves from that disempowering belief.

We'll get into the process of how you can liberate yourself from your own limiting beliefs, but the first stage – awareness – is recognizing that within you is an inner compass that helps you navigate from where you've been to where you want to be. The first awareness was the law of vibration and understanding that everything in this universe is law-based. Like the universe, the brain also operates in a very specific way, and understanding how the mind works helps us eliminate superstitious beliefs that we're often tripping over as we try to create positive changes.

So Much More than Affirmations

Let me take a moment to talk about something very important that's a common misunderstanding when we talk about the law of vibration and subsequently the law of attraction. When someone is trying to manifest their dream business, a million dollars, or whatever their goal is, they have an assumption that all they have to do is say what they want. "I just have to affirm it over and over and over again." While we do condition our subconscious minds with repetition, **the real key is repetition with the correct emotional state**, and therefore a vibration that matches what we want. When most people are thinking about that million dollars they want, they're actually in the mental-emotional-vibrational state of lack because they're not attending to the negative emotion they're feeling.

Let's go back to the example of the person who wants to lose 20 pounds. If they become aware of the negative feeling associated with that thought, then they can look at what they're actually thinking about it. You can see there's a discrepancy between their desired outcome (20 pounds lighter) and their current beliefs. Their current beliefs are causing a lower vibrational emotion. What they're emitting mentally-emotionally-vibrationally is not 20 pounds lighter. It's "I can't be 20 pounds lighter." In the example of wanting to manifest a million dollars, while they think, "I'm a millionaire, I'm a millionaire, I'm so happy and grateful that I'm now a millionaire," if they're aware of what they're actually *feeling*, they're probably not emitting the vibration of having a million dollars. More often than not, they're emitting the vibration that matches their current beliefs – "I don't have a million dollars yet, and I don't know where it will come from." Notice how that feels. It doesn't not feel like abundance, nor does it feel like being a millionaire.

> *For affirmations to have any impact, you must also feel the right emotions, and be in the correct vibrational state.*

Instead, imagine what it would feel like to have that million dollars in the bank and give yourself permission to explore in your mind that emotional state. How would it feel to have one million dollars? That feels much different from simply affirming, "I am a millionaire." If you can affirm your goal and actually trigger the associated thought and feeling of "it's a done deal and is real and it feels good," then it's beneficial. You will be successfully using the law of attraction to your advantage.

Our inner work is to train our mind to feel the certainty of having what we want (belief vs. doubt). If you think about something you want that you do not have, notice the feeling of lack it evokes. If you think about something you have that you love or enjoy, notice the feeling of abundance or gratitude it evokes. The *feeling of having* also feels very natural, like a sense of certainty. That is essentially the state we want to get ourselves into when we think about our goals. Even those things that we don't have yet, but just know we will have, evokes that sense of certainty. We've all had experiences of knowing that we will have something we really desire. Recall that feeling and bring it into your conscious awareness when you envision your current goal.

As a brief aside, you need to understand that your beliefs and your emotional state are a precursor to the actions that you take to achieve your desired goal. So, what we are talking about here is much more substantial than simply putting desires on your vision board or visualizing your goals. *Without the right mindset, you simply will not be aligned with the actions that move you toward your desired outcome.* Your mindset is determined by your beliefs, attitude, and emotional state… and your mindset is directly linked to your vibrational point of attraction.

Awareness is understanding how the universe operates, understanding what we're doing in any given moment in terms of our own vibrational point of attraction, and feeling the subtle distinctions between when we're in alignment with our goals and desires versus being out of alignment based on the way it feels. This emotional guidance system (taught very well by Abraham-Hicks) is our ability, through the process of our own awareness, sometimes referred to as mindfulness, to feel when we are pointed in the wrong direction. This awareness or mindfulness is an indicator of when we need to shift our thinking or when we need to be really honest about what our actual beliefs are on any given subject, so we can challenge and then shift those beliefs. Throughout this book, I'll be teaching you ways to identify your limiting beliefs and old disempowering patterns, and what you can do to shift those and properly release them, allowing you to move into alignment and congruence with what your heart desires.

A quick tip for "challenging" your old beliefs: Remember, our programmed beliefs are powerful, and the longer you've reinforced an old limiting belief, the more difficult it can be to objectively see that we can in fact change it, and our circumstances. When you notice a negative emotion and acknowledge the thoughts that are causing it, ask yourself the following questions:

1) Does this belief help me or anyone else in any truly positive, meaningful way?
2) Is this belief a universal truth that applies to everyone?

Let's break this down further: First, when you honestly assess whether the belief truly serves you and others in a positive way, you'll notice that limiting beliefs are never higher truths. In fact, if you are honest and objective, you'll identify better ways to think about, feel and/or approach virtually any situation. This is important because if a limiting belief is unchallenged, the mind will continue to default to the old, programmed response. To liberate yourself from old patterns, you must demonstrate to your mind that there is a better way.

Second, when you challenge the validity of a belief, your mind will be open to a higher truth. We tend to accept our beliefs as the only truth for us, unless and until we clearly see that it is in fact just a belief. I frequently say, "If it is not a law of the universe, then it is just a belief, and beliefs can be changed." Consider for a moment that thing that you've been struggling with; if it is nothing more than a belief – and you can change it – then what else is possible for you? As I just stated, beliefs left unchallenged will continue to control you. When you shine the light of truth on an old, accepted belief, you have the power to change it.

True Desires

The third piece of awareness is a very important part of my ALIGN process. I'll be diving into it deeper later in the book but allow me to touch on it now. It's the awareness of what our heart truly desires. A lot of people are setting goals and living life in a way that's incongruent with what they really and truly desire. When we see images or read marketing pieces that promote a certain lifestyle – working only a few hours a week, owning a 10,000-square-foot home, a garage full of expensive cars, we can become confused because those things generate a certain excitement. It feels liberating and empowering, so we believe that we must have those things to enjoy the good feelings the images initially generated. However, we're failing to recognize that what we actually desire is the essence of the freedom, the empowerment, and having things that we love... although not necessarily the specific manifestations we see in the marketing images.

As a result, people are setting goals that are based on what they associate with success rather than their authentic desires, so they are not truly inspired as they pursue the goal. They're setting goals for things they think they're supposed to want because they've made a mental association between those things and success and freedom. The issue with this is twofold. First, when someone sets this type of goal, they are much more likely to give up when they encounter resistance, which creates negative patterns in the mind that they are a failure, don't have what it takes, etc. Second, if the goal is achieved, there is usually a feeling of emptiness or disappointment that follows because there was a lack of passion in pursuit of the goal.

This portion of awareness is recognizing when our goal (what we think we want) isn't really what we want, so we can gain clarity on what we do really desire which will give us the most joy, the most fulfillment, the most passion, and the most meaning in our lives. This is what we're all reaching for. It's the feeling of success and freedom; it's those higher vibrational emotions. We want material things to be a vibrational match to those feelings.

Now, it is not always the case that your goals are completely misaligned with your authentic desires. However, even misalignment caused by disempowering old programming can create problems. Over the many years that I've been working with clients, it's common for new clients to come to me making the statement, "I feel unfulfilled when I achieve my goals." They expect to feel better, especially when they achieve a big goal they've set, so they think something is wrong with them because they aren't living happily ever after. They feel empty after achieving a big financial milestone. This comes right back to understanding that we live in a law-based universe with an emotional guidance system and a need to identify our true hearts' desires *and* align ourselves mentally and emotionally with them.

> *Your emotional vibrational state when pursuing any goal affects your fulfillment when you achieve it.*

When I work with these new clients, I'm helping them identify what they were actually feeling – what they were vibrating – while they were in pursuit of creating that particular goal. Most times, they'll acknowledge that they were not in a very high vibrational state. Instead, they were feeling stress and anxiety. The desire was something they thought would make them happy; however, they were not in a happy state while they were taking the steps to achieve that goal or outcome.

When you try to manifest something to make yourself feel better, you're operating out of alignment with the way the universe works. This is the way most people are working. Conversely, when you recognize that you can feel throughout your journey whether you are in harmony with what you're trying to achieve, it impacts your happiness and fulfillment. When you're feeling a lot of anxiety and stress, you are in a negative state, so ask yourself, "Is this something I want to create more of?" No doubt, your answer will be no, so ask what you'd prefer. How would you prefer to feel as you are taking action to create your million dollars?

If you can feel how you want to feel *while* you are creating your million dollars, then when you create that big manifestation, you've already primed your mind to feel the positive emotions you want to feel. It's partially about conditioning your subconscious mind to feel how you want to feel and partially in accordance with the vibrational law of attraction. Like attracts like, so you need to be a vibrational match to what you want and how you want to feel.

A lot of people get confused about the correlation between emotions and manifestations. When they initially learn about the law of attraction or hear things about the importance of positivity, they assume positive thinking and a happy disposition are required to achieve wealth and success. However, there are plenty of people who've been able to create financially lucrative businesses who are miserable and operating with a very negative mindset. How is that possible? Picture Ebeneezer Scrooge. That's the person who's financially well off but always in a negative state. The reason? It's the way the universe works. You can create money and still feel negative emotions. **If you believe you can create money, you can create money.** But if you're feeling negative the whole time, when the money comes, you'll still feel negative emotions. Just because you have the money doesn't mean the negative feelings go away. In essence, you get the vibrational equivalent of all your predominant beliefs, expectations, and feelings.

We can create seemingly great things in our lives and not enjoy them. Why? We have not been mentally, emotionally and vibrationally attuned to the way we want to feel. **A big part of creating a life that is really, truly fulfilling and meaningful is retraining ourselves to be in the emotional vibrational state that we want to embody as our predominant state of being.** And we must create the manifestations from this same place. The manifestation, in and of itself, cannot change your emotional state because it has not been a practiced state. The dream house will never give you happily ever after if you're not a mental and emotional match to feeling happily ever after. Yes, you can manifest the house, but you'll still feel the same old way you did before you achieved it.

If we can challenge your old beliefs and raise your emotional vibrational state, conditioning ourselves with beliefs that feel more congruent, harmonious, and empowering, then we're creating in harmony with the laws of the universe. Understanding how the universe operates and how our minds work, now we're in a place to create an empowering, fulfilling, and positive life!

Highlights About "Awareness"

- Everything has its own vibrational frequency, including thoughts and emotions.

- Feelings are indicators as to whether or not we are in harmony with what we want.
- Your limiting beliefs prevent you from what you really want.
- Limiting beliefs lie deep in your subconscious mind, and most people don't realize there is something they can do to clean them up.
- For affirmations to have any impact, you must also be in the right vibrational frequency by feeling the right emotions.
- Your emotional state when setting and pursuing any goal affects your fulfillment when you achieve it.
- Success and fulfillment are not mutually linked. Many people achieve incredible successes without ever feeling good about them.
- A big part of creating a life that is really, truly fulfilling and meaningful is retraining ourselves to be in the emotional vibrational state that we want to embody as our predominant state of being.

Chapter Two

Learn

Throughout the entire ALIGN process, learning will always be occurring, but in the beginning, clients have to learn how to release negative emotions and identify and shift limiting beliefs, bad habits, and old subconscious programs. The thing I want you to remember is that you do not develop mastery simply by learning a technique. As with any other skill, you must practice the technique to be able to use it as a skill that becomes highly effective.

I know there are a lot of people teaching modalities, and there are a lot of people looking at modalities as a "one size fits all" solution to every problem. That's simply not the case. While we use modalities like hypnosis, EFT, and various mindset techniques (including neurolinguistic programming), we need to remember that the modality is simply a tool. A hammer is also a tool, but you know that it cannot solve every building problem. It's the perfect tool for driving nails and can be a valuable, critical tool; however, it's only one tool. Throughout the journey we're going to take to shifting old patterns and reconditioning our minds to support us in achieving all our goals and dreams, we'll use modalities as tools, not as a holy grail or magic bullet.

We also want to be sure that as we're learning to use these different modalities, we remember the fundamental principles about how the mind and the universe work. The modality – the tool – will only get you so far. I see a lot of people only giving lip service to their goals without being a vibrational match. For many people, they're going through the motions without being dialed in to the process that needs to occur for the modality to be effective. This is why I frequently remind my clients when using EFT or releasing exercises to be very **honest** with themselves about what they are thinking and feeling.

For example, I used EFT to work through a lot of deep-rooted limiting beliefs, but I learned that if I was not in the right mindset (just going through the motions), the technique was not particularly effective. However, when I went through the process being in the right mindset and focusing on the core principles that we are covering in this book, the technique was incredibly useful. As I work with clients, I'm continuously reminding them about these fundamental principles. Mastering the fundamentals is an essential part of this learning process.

Universal principles are basic facts of life that seem so obvious once you learn them, but they're not taught in school or by parents and you don't know to be aware of these things, so we default to less-than-ideal beliefs that are often perpetuating, not solving, your problems. Even after we've experienced an ah-ha moment, we can easily resort to old habits. Rather than beat yourself up when you fall back into negative habits of thought or behavior, appreciate your awareness of it and gently guide yourself through the processes you're learning in this book.

Identify and Release

One of the first things I want to focus on as part of the learning process is identifying and releasing fear and other heavy emotional energies. Fear is one of the most common sticking points for eliminating limiting beliefs. Fear is a powerful negative emotion that can block even the most positive intention. When we release it, we can neutralize the associated mental program, so it no longer pulls us into the old default pattern.

There are many techniques for releasing, and they're effective because they enable you to release stored up, negative emotion (a.k.a. energy). I personally like to teach my clients a very simple releasing process that works for virtually everyone. When you are aware of a negative feeling, remember that emotion is energy. Energy is in a constant state of motion, and it will flow out of the body if we are not unconsciously repressing it. So, **begin by allowing yourself to feel the negative emotion, and intentionally give yourself permission to let it come up and allow it to pass through.** Some people naturally feel as though they are breathing it out, while other visualize or imagine the energy rising up and out through the top of their head.

I encourage you to practice this right now. Think of a challenge in your life. Notice the negative emotions that arise and be mindful of how it physically feels in your body. Now, set the intention to allow the feeling to flow up and out. Give yourself permission to say "yes" to letting the energy come up and pass through. As long as you continue to feel the physical and/or emotional sensations, continue to invite them up and intentionally allow the feelings to pass through. You should begin to feel relief. Keep in mind, there is no right or wrong way to experience this. Everyone is unique. The objective is to use the power of your intention to allow the feelings to pass through, so you are naturally releasing and letting them go.

Think about that same challenge again. Does it feel less emotionally charged? If so, great! If not, go through the process again. You may notice some different thoughts coming up this time that have a lot of negative emotional charge. If so, stay mindful and intentional, allow those feelings to rise up and be released. Either breathing out the energy or releasing it through the top of your head like smoke rising up and dissipating into the air.

For many of our negative thoughts, this simple releasing process works wonderfully. For our more complicated issues, we need to be much more mindful of deeper-rooted fears, insecurities, limiting beliefs, and the habit of feeling like a victim. While we can release all of those associated negative emotions with this process, techniques like EFT (Emotional Freedom Techniques) can be more efficient for some people.

Keep in mind that we don't simply store negative emotions; we can also store positive emotions, and both can generate powerful associations. Most of the time our positive associations are not an issue, but in some instances they are. For example, if someone is addicted to smoking, they have strong emotional associations with that behavior, some of which appear to be positive in nature, like taking a break from work. If someone associates releasing stress with smoking a cigarette during a break, there's a positive feeling that has an adverse effect. The person is attached to a behavior that is harmful because it's also carrying a positive association – taking a break and relieving stress.

When we identify these emotional triggers and emotionally charged associations, we must be willing to release feelings linked to the patterns, behaviors, and beliefs, so we can more objectively examine the behavior and make a more empowering choice. For the smoker who wants to quit, if they're objective rather than emotionally

> *As long as there is a strong negative emotional charge with any association, you will be stuck in the old pattern.*

charged, they may be able to realize that smoking is not necessary to achieve the desired result – stress relief by taking a break. They may need to find a suitable replacement, like taking a walk or enjoyable reading. Of course, it will be unique for everyone, and the key is that the replacement feels good, so there is more value in the new association and behavior than there was with the old one.

As long as there is a strong emotional charge with the old association, whether positive or negative, they'll be stuck in the old pattern. With this example, a fear of loss of the benefit (stress relief) will cause the mind to hold on to the old negative behavior. This is why it is so important to look at all of our beliefs around the pattern we want to change.

A process that I frequently teach in my group programs to help identify limiting beliefs and disempowering associations is to sit quietly with a pen and paper and write out everything you believe about your goal and your ability to achieve it. Self-honesty is the key here, so you need to write everything down that comes into your conscious awareness. We have a tendency to dismiss thoughts that we object to. However, you need to remember, if it is coming up, then it is in your subconscious mind. We want to address all of those programmed beliefs, so they no longer adversely affect you.

Once you've purged all those thoughts, beliefs, and associations from your mind and have them on paper, now you can work through them with EFT, or release the negative emotions by seeing them objectively and allowing the feelings they evoke to pass through.

With that, let's return to my statement about fear. Fear is often entangled with many of our attachments to limiting beliefs and old patterns. When we set an intention to release the feelings associated with those beliefs, we may notice a fear surrounding that release. Be mindful that even though your mind is attempting to protect you through fear-based thoughts, there's always a better way to think and feel about virtually any subject. From our earlier discussion about the law of attraction, you understand that like attracts like. When you're in the vibration of fear, it's a very low vibrational frequency. Not only does fear adversely affect you vibrationally by drawing more thoughts and circumstances into your life that match the vibration of fear, but it also has an adverse effect on your mindset, and therefore your actions (or in many instances, your reactions). It's not productive, and there's always a better way to perceive a circumstance than staying stuck in fear.

When I'm working with someone who has a challenge like OCD and they're obsessed with cleaning, they usually acknowledge it's an unhealthy pattern or behavior, but the mind can be very black-and-white in its thinking making it difficult to change the behavior. The mind is often convinced that if we release an unhealthy attachment to a behavior, that we will experience the extreme opposite, which is what we don't want.

In this example, the person truly likes the sensation of a clean home, but the mind cannot let go of the attachment to the obsessive behavior because the person fears they will stop caring about the cleanliness of their home and will end up living in a dirty, unkept home which does not feel good. In its black-and-white approach, the mind does not allow for the idea that the person can still be cleanly without an obsessive quality. For instance, "I can be more relaxed about this and still have a clean home." Remember that once your mind locks into any pattern, it does not want to let go because of fear, even though that fear tends to be irrational.

Releasing Is Natural

This is why releasing negative emotion – in this case, fear – is so critical. You can let the feeling come up and then allow it to pass through, whether breathing it out with intention or visualizing fear as energy leaving your body. Releasing energy is a natural occurrence. We do it all day... except on our emotionally triggered hang ups. Admit to yourself, "I am feeling this fear about..." along with a willingness to release that low vibrational energy. When you make a mindful decision to release the energy, you'll be able to get that energy flowing.

> *Releasing a feeling is the key to gaining greater objectivity about it.*

Another helpful process to let go of the stuck emotional energy is to pause, close your eyes, and focus on deep intentional breaths. Mindful breathing helps regulate the nervous system, and it allows intense energy to dissipate. It seems so simple; it is easy to discredit its effectiveness. However, you can feel the physiological shift and the emotional relief when you do this practice. As we'll get into a little later in the book, our ability to shift old beliefs and behaviors is largely dependent on being a receptive reprogramming state. The ability to release intense negative emotions is extremely valuable.

We tend to want to push negative emotion away or suppress or ignore it. Even when you try to positive self-talk your way out of it, the energy remains stuck, which is why dysfunctional feelings continue to be triggered. Make a conscious choice to release the feeling, and in the process of doing so, you'll begin to neutralize the associated emotion from the belief or pattern.

Once you release the emotional charge (and for some issues, there will be many beliefs with negative associations), you'll be able to objectively see that there is a better way to feel and to perceive the circumstance. And once you see that, you'll realize you can choose a more empowering association that you can begin to anchor into your subconscious mind. As an example, if someone is afraid of heights, we know there's a better way to feel about heights than simply being in a state of extreme fear. Just because the person releases the fear does not mean they'll become reckless and decide to step off a two-story building. They'll still practice proper caution but will be able to do so more objectively and more calmly. The intense negative emotion will be gone. Once they release fear, they can more objectively ask, "How would I prefer to feel?" This is the next step in the learn process. We don't simply release, release, release. We have to reprogram.

Reprogram

Reprogramming requires a lot of self-discipline. Plenty of people will acknowledge their uncomfortable feelings, but then forget that they must reach for a more empowering thought and feeling to replace the old, negative ones.

In the case of the fear of heights, once the negatively charged emotion is released, now they can (and must) reach for a better association. They might reach for calm, envisioning themselves at the window of a ten-story building feeling calm, relaxed, and in control of their mental and emotional state. They're creating something new in their mind. This is the beginning of reprogramming the mind.

A lot of people try to reprogram without cleaning up the old negative associations. It's possible with very long-term, consistent repetition, but it's inefficient. Instead, when you release the old negative emotions associated with memories and limiting beliefs, and intentionally replace those old associations with something more empowering, you'll find you'll be much more productive.

This is no different from trying to use positive affirmations to overcome an issue about which you have a lot of limiting beliefs. Again, you can say a positive affirmation all day long, but if you feel like what you're saying is complete b/s, you'll gain nothing. You cannot simultaneously think and feel the opposite of your affirmation and expect positive results because you are still carrying too much negative emotional charge. Your predominant mental-emotional-vibrational state is negative – exactly what you don't want more of. If this is what's happening with your attempts at affirmation, you're doing yourself a disservice. Every time you state your affirmation, you'll be activating your old program and negative beliefs, practicing that vibration instead.

> *Successful and effective reprogramming only happens after you've removed the negative associations first.*

When we're aware of the negative feeling, we can mindfully use the process of releasing and reprogramming. Give yourself permission to recognize the feeling as energy that was triggered and acknowledge that you feel it, then allow the feeling to arise and pass through. Do this as an objective observer – observing yourself experiencing the negative emotional charge. The feeling comes up and passes through, and the result should be a sense of relief and a more neutral emotional state. Now consider: *"How would I prefer to feel about this? What positive association do I want instead?"* What improved thought can you have about this subject that feels better? Imagine that improved circumstance and notice how it feels.

At this point, a lot of people make the mistake of jumping to an ideal circumstance or a big goal from that low vibrational state, but in many cases, it's still too far from their active vibration, so the positive emotion is unsustainable. *You must be mindful of what feels better than what you were just thinking yet is still believable and acceptable to your mind*, so you can get into that emotional vibration state and stay there. Yes, you can ultimately achieve resonance with the big goal or ideal state, but it may be a process of steps to get there. Imagine a staircase. You can't get to the top in one leap. You take one step at a time. Energy works the same way. We'll get deeper into the emotional vibrational spectrum later in the book, but for now, just remember that what you are reaching for is an improved way of thinking about and feeling about the subject.

Essentially, when we think about an improved situation, we are visualizing or imaging it. Visualization is an effective way of getting yourself mentally and emotionally into your preferred state. And it is a powerful way to program your subconscious mind. You have many opportunities throughout the day to go through "mini reprograms." You do this by recognizing an old negative emotion and, in the moment, release it, and shift into what you'd prefer by visualizing or imagining it and feeling as though you are experiencing it right now. Doing this imprints on the subconscious mind, and it's like a mini self-hypnosis session. **Repetition and positive emotions create new and empowering subconscious programs.**

Let's look at an example, if you want to grow your business but have bumped into self-doubt or failure to achieve desired results (a belief that "everything I try doesn't work"), when you see an opportunity, be aware of the associated negative emotion. Let's say a marketing opportunity comes up, but you default to your old belief that it won't work. The negative emotion is your indicator to begin your mini reprogram – release the negative emotional charge and imprint your mind with a new belief and association. Feel the old negative feeling and allow it to pass through. Don't ignore it but don't dwell on it. Instead of repressing, let it come all the way to the surface and experience the relief of releasing it, and in the state of relief, now ask, "What would I prefer?"

In the case of the marketing opportunity, perhaps you want to feel more optimistic. "There's a learning curve, but it can work out for me." You've shifted your emotional state, now let's take it a step further, "I would prefer to create a very successful marketing campaign that allows growth with more ease." That is a progressively positive thought and emotion and you are moving in the right direction. But we need to give it more than lip service. So, **take a few moments to impress upon your subconscious what it actually looks and feels like**. Visualize or imagine what experiences you will you have when you have the desired outcome and notice how good it feels.

I can assure you that in the past, you've been visualizing what you didn't want to happen (for example, when you worry about something). Look for these opportunities throughout your day to flip it and visualize what you'd prefer. When you allow yourself to feel positive emotions, you're imprinting that on your subconscious mind. First, break the habit of defaulting to the negative association by acknowledging the emotion. By doing so, you stop the energetic loop and can release the old emotional charge. Then you intentionally change your emotional vibration state by allowing yourself to imagine and feel the preferred state and result. In so doing, you recondition your subconscious mind with what you want to experience and change your vibrational point of attraction.

What we believe (what we've imprinted on our subconscious mind that matches our expectations) combined with our vibrational point of attraction is what we experience in life. If you want to be metaphysical about this, you can see the benefit of placing yourself in vibrational resonance with what you want. If you want to be more practical about it, you can see that if your mind is conditioned to believe and expect you can be successful, you're going to begin to take the appropriate steps to get the outcomes you want. Whether you're spiritual or highly pragmatic, you can see this process is incredibly valuable to creating the right mindset and emotional vibrational state to move in the direction of where you want to go.

From my experience working with business owners, the ability to reprogram our thoughts and beliefs proves to be one of the first – and most powerful – turning points for my clients. While I'm confident that the steps you've read in this section can begin to produce some great results for you, obviously the results you may experience will come faster and be more dramatic when you have expert support.

Highlights About "Learn"

- Modalities are tools, and no one tool fixes every problem.
- We store emotions – both negative and positive, so identifying them is the starting point, keeping in mind that bad habits (like smoking) can also carry a positive association (break from stress).

- Your mind tends to be very black-and-white in thinking without allowing for nuances that actually exist.
- Releasing energy is a natural occurrence, but when it comes to our hang ups and limiting beliefs, we must be more mindful and intentional about it.
- Releasing fear or any negative emotion does not mean that you'll become reckless. It will allow you to become more objective.
- Successful and effective reprogramming only happens after you've removed the negative associations first.
- When you feel negative emotions, recognizing them for what they are, and allow them to pass through, you'll feel a sense of relief and be able to recondition yourself with a more preferable association.
- Look for opportunities throughout the day to apply "mini reprograms," taking a few moments to recognize, release, and ask what you'd prefer to feel or experience.
- Your stated preference will only be lip service unless you take a few moments to visualize or imagine what it will look and feel like.

At this point, I want to take a moment to encourage you to go deeper into learning the various tools and processes I've touched on. My Business Mastery Academy is designed to help you learn and master the various tools I have referenced throughout this chapter, which can assist you with releasing and reprogramming your mind. Within the Academy are basic and advanced trainings on the modalities, EFT videos, Releasing processes, Hypnosis audios, Meditations and other resources to support you.

Get your first month of the Academy for free; and if you decide to continue after the trial period, you are welcome to cancel anytime.

Start your free month at: www.acintl.us

Chapter Three
Identify

While I've covered the need to identify and recognize your limiting beliefs and fears, in this part of the ALIGN process, we will also get into identifying your true heart's desires. Our authentic – true heart's – desires sometimes differ from goals that you set for yourself. Many entrepreneurs perceive success a certain way, with an idea of success that is often influenced by what they've seen and heard, including aspirations of other people they admire. It might be the mansion, the cars, the bank account. In many cases, we're setting both business and life goals that are somewhat superficial.

If we do the inner work I've been teaching you to this point (cleaning up our misaligned limiting beliefs and focusing on what we'd prefer), we'll begin to recognize that some of our goals and aspirations are probably not even what we want. In pursuit of these, "checking off the box," and stacking up accolades to gratify the ego, we'll feel an emptiness because we're not congruent with our true heart's desire. A lot of people are reaching for the money, success, or status to attempt to feel better, more confident, worthier, or more significant. "When I have the thing, I'll finally feel good enough." Achieving the goal without the feeling you want creates additional conflict in your heart and mind.

Throughout our journey, we're cleaning up misperceptions and false ideas about what it will take for us to feel good enough and fulfilled, and we're creating more clarity and meaning as we're pursuing heartfelt desires. Clients ask me, "How do I distinguish between an authentic desire and something I believe I want?" In many cases, it's not that you're completely off base, it's that you're slightly skewed because of your limiting beliefs, need for approval, and fears, doubts and insecurities. There's some lower vibrational stuff that becomes part of your motivation.

For example, there's nothing wrong with wanting a successful business. There are so many positive intentions behind that desire. However, we need to clean up the superficial motivations, so you can be more congruent, high vibrational, and aligned with your desire. When we're moving toward goal fulfillment and actively cleaning up the lower vibrational stuff and frequently in a higher vibrational state, we're naturally feeling good, positive emotions. This brings a greater sense of fulfillment in our day-to-day lives. We'll also feel so much better when we achieve the goal because we've been practicing the mental-emotional-vibrational state of congruence and alignment.

From this state, our actions are more inspired and aligned with our values; they're emanating from a better mindset. The outcomes are then much more positive. This doesn't mean you won't encounter challenges. Yes, you're going to notice old fears, doubts, and limiting beliefs, which is why it's important to practice awareness and use the processes, mindful of the fundamental principles I've covered. Awareness helps you have more clarity than ever before about when you are focusing on the wrong things, so you can refocus on what you want instead.

> *The more positive we feel on our journey, the clearer and more aligned we'll be with what we're ultimately working toward.*

For instance, if you're working on your business, doing various tasks intended to help you achieve your desired outcome, you may notice some negative emotions. These indicate that you're *thinking* about something you don't want or like... actually projecting a negative outcome into your future. Maybe you're worrying about not getting the result you want or that people are going to judge you. The negative emotion is your indicator that, in that moment, your vibrational point of attraction is a low frequency and not at all what you want to create.

Putting it into practice: Be mindful of this state, and actively and with intention, release the negative emotional charge. This may mean examining that which you fear – those deep-rooted limiting beliefs, as we covered in the previous chapter. If your mind resurrects memories of times when you've taken a similar step and something bad happened (lost money, faced criticism, etc.), even though you know you must do this activity, you're triggered with fear, and now you have split energy. As you're in conflict with yourself, pulled in different directions, you're lowering to a more negative vibrational point of attraction. It adversely affects your feelings, including the quality of your actions and the quality of your mood. The result is almost always a less-than-desirable outcome.

Objectively recognize this feeling is just old energy and let it come up and pass through. Release and let go. As you're willing to be honest with yourself about your resistance to the activity and clear it away, remember the next step is to ask how you'd prefer to feel about it and/or what you'd prefer to experience. Then allow yourself to actually feel those positive emotions. By exercising this mental muscle, you're getting yourself into a positive feeling state. You're changing and raising your vibration. In that moment, you're reprogramming your subconscious mind and creating a new frame of reference.

In hypnosis, we refer to this as creating a new "known." You are always operating subconsciously on "knowns." Knowns are our conditioned habits, beliefs, and associations. Basically, it's anything that has been put into the subconscious mind, whether real or imagined, that we default to. Replacing old, unsupportive knowns with new ones that do support you is the goal. Your mind does not differentiate between what is real (has physically manifested) and what is imagined. So, impress upon your mind a new positive image of what you want with a positive feeling in order to anchor it into your subconscious and allow it to be your new known. The more often you do this, the more you reinforce this mental conditioning and the more it becomes your default. I'm sure you can see how this is beneficial in pursuit of your goals. As we're gaining clarity on what we truly want, now we have a map to guide us to each correct next step.

> *Your mind does not differentiate between what is real and what is imagined. You have the power to imagine what you want, and program your mind to support you in achieving it.*

Higher Calling and Purpose

Let's consider what I call your higher or divine calling and what that has to do with your goals, dreams, and heart's desires. Many people use the phrase "life's purpose," and while they get it conceptually, they don't really know what it means to them. A lot of people associate "meaning" and "purpose" with this really big mission, operating at a level of someone who's impacting millions of other people. However, not all our inner and higher callings are necessarily these grandiose things.

Our divine inner calling shows up as our heart's desires – both big and small. When you're in alignment with what your heart desires, notice that you're a wonderful version of yourself. Maybe that's being a loving and compassionate parent, a successful entrepreneur doing work that benefits others whether on a large or small scale, or simply being a kind person helping someone who's having a challenge. Even the littlest things make a difference and give our lives so much more meaning.

If you're only looking for meaning through your business, you're missing out on incredible richness and fulfillment! Our calling to be a better person is divine. Our calling to be more authentic and congruent with ourselves in our businesses is also divine. Anytime your heart has a desire, and you question how it could possibly be divine, I want you to remember that you are essentially a divine being, having a human experience.

If your heart desires a new luxury car with all the extra features, your ego may tell you, "That's not a divine calling; that's simply an ego desire. You don't need that thing and it's only a gratification want." I'm going to challenge that voice. If your heart desires something that is not harming anyone else, but is, in fact, raising your vibration, that's a beautiful and wonderful thing. We have to look at our desires differently.

Part of your motivation for the fancy car may be coming from a superficial place, a desire for someone else's approval, or compensation for a feeling of unworthiness. These are instances in which you have to go back and use the tools to clean up these lower vibrational patterns. Now you can see how this comes full circle.

There's an ongoing process:
- Be mindful and aware of what you're feeling.
- Notice lower vibrational cues.
- Use your tools to clean up these lower vibrational emotions, beliefs, patterns, and behaviors.
- Reach for the improved thought and feeling. "What would I prefer?"
- Visualize or imagine and feel what you want to experience instead that is more positive and empowering.

For example, if you feel a little guilty about wanting that nice car, do your inner work to examine your beliefs about that emotion. "I have some shame about this." Now release the negative emotional charge with that old association. Then reprogram yourself with a more empowering association, "I'd prefer to know that I am absolutely worthy of nice things. It feels self-loving and respectful to own the type of car I prefer." Get yourself mentally-emotionally to the place where you can have a beautiful car and feel good. I want you to drive that car, not with a feeling of egotistical pride, but with a sense of joyful alignment that represents your preference.

With this approach, you're designing your life more congruently, saying yes to your heart's desires and knowing that when you do, you are being a higher vibrational version of yourself.

Self-Honesty

As we continue on this journey, I encourage you to be mindful of where and when you trip over your own lower vibrational beliefs. Your work is the inner work – being aware of your feelings and knowing that your emotions are neither inherently good nor bad, right nor wrong. They are indicators of where you're focused and your level of congruence with yourself.

Putting into practice what I covered with you so far, I want you to notice – **identify** – the things you desire for yourself. What are some of the goals you have for yourself and what are your motivations behind those goals? You'll notice that some of your motivations are positive, and you feel good about them. You'll also notice that other motivators carry lower vibrations because they're coming from fears, doubts, insecurities, and old limiting beliefs. As mentioned briefly earlier, it is very common that some of your goals may be purely superficial. We tend to try to overcompensate for our insecurities by achieving things we believe will make us feel better. Begin by looking at the motivations behind each of your goals honestly and objectively, then use the process to release and reprogram, so you can move forward toward your authentic goals in a more empowered way.

By evaluating your goals honestly, you may notice that you don't even truly want some of the things you've been working toward. You may also notice that you are really passionate about certain things but have been holding yourself back because of fears, self-doubt, and old limiting beliefs. As you continue to do your inner work, utilizing the shifting process I keep encouraging you to do, you will get more and more clear about what you truly want and aligned with creating it in your life.

Highlights About "Identify"

- There's a difference between setting a goal and pursuing your true heart's desire.
- The more positive we feel on our journey, the clearer and more aligned we'll be on what we're ultimately working toward.
- A negative emotion is your indicator that, in that moment, your vibrational point of attraction is a low frequency and not at all what you want to create.
- Your mind does not differentiate between what is real and what is imagined. You have the power to program your mind by visualizing and feeling what you want.
- Not all of your higher callings must be grandiose. Even the littlest things make a difference and give our lives so much more meaning.
- Whenever your heart's desire is something that raises your vibration, it's wonderful and, in fact, divine.
- Emotions are never right nor wrong, good nor bad, they indicate where you're focused and your level of congruence with yourself.

Within your Academy membership, you'll find guided hypnosis audios, and several trainings that are designed to help you clarify and align with your heart's desires and purpose. Usually, we have some degree of awareness about our higher calling, but it is not unusual for old limiting beliefs to interfere with our clarity and self-belief. If you struggle in this area, be sure to locate the resources inside of the Academy to support you. Start your free month at: www.acintl.us

Identify

Chapter Four
Gain Momentum

Now it's time to take the next step: gain momentum. On one hand, this is the most exciting part of the process; however, there is a caveat. As we experience positive evidence of the work we're doing, there are going to be highs... and lows.

Let's start for a moment with the high moments because it's probably the reason you're reading this book. You have goals, dreams, and awareness of your heart's desires. You're willing to do the inner work to create the business – and life – you love. Through this process of identifying those limiting beliefs, being aware of the lower vibrational indicators, cleaning up your energy and raising your vibration, and reprogramming your subconscious mind, of course you'll see positive evidence of your efforts. Sometimes, there will be small breakthroughs and ah-ha moments when you feel an emotional shift on something that may have been a challenge or a trigger for you before.

There are also going to be big, wonderful manifestations when you see your lofty goals and desires come into full fruition. This is exciting to experience! Yet, you are still a human being (just like the rest of us) who's still full of subconscious conditioning from a lifetime of some good and probably a lot of not-so-good programming that you'll bump up against on your journey. This is especially common when you're reaching for the new and unknown.

Tripping Points Along the Way

I'm sure you've heard the personal development cliché about "getting outside of your comfort zone." In other words, anytime you reach for the unknown that's new to your subconscious mind, your mind will start firing warning bells: "This is not who we are; this is not what we do!" The result is resistance and fear, showing you your own limiting beliefs around the topic, as well as your current self-image. It will uncover your unhealed and unaddressed emotional wounds and those insidious insecurities that cause you to seek others' approval. They may be financial insecurities or even more deep-seated ones regarding survival. Because you will encounter these things as you reach for your next level of success in any area of your business or life, I want to address them in this chapter.

Some of the old limiting beliefs will be easy for you to shift and you'll be able to keep moving forward with positive momentum. However, there are a couple of growth-related obstacles that frequently occur, and it's very valuable to be aware of these, so they don't stop you dead in your tracks. The first phenomenon is sometimes referred to as "new level, new devil" or your "upper limit problem." I'm talking about what happens when you reach for something completely new that often contradicts your old self-image, and it stirs up all sorts of fears, doubts, insecurities, and limiting beliefs that cause you emotional distress. When this occurs, you'll notice a lot of negative thoughts and feelings that may feel uncontrollable. You may even experience negative manifestations – obstacles in your life and business.

> *"New level, new devil" often arises as you reach for the new and unknown.*

When this occurs, you might think the universe is saying "no" to you or that you just don't have what it takes, but what's really happening is your unresolved triggers are causing you to be a vibrational match to those old, unwanted patterns. *Remember, we create what we believe and expect. We create a life that matches our self-image. We draw into our lives circumstances that feel similar to our active vibration.* Stop and do your inner work to clean up this negative energy. These old patterns, behaviors, and habits are incongruent with who you are reaching to become and what you aspire to create in your life and business!

Many of the greatest leaders in personal development and business motivation talk about the importance of persistence. **Persistence is a state of mind.** Just keep in mind, (rather than purely pushing through resistance, doubt, and fear) I want you to intentionally look at your beliefs so you can release and reprogram. Set yourself up for success instead of struggle.

Why Obstacles Show Up

Hitting your self-imposed upper limit can show up anytime you are expanding into the new and unknown. The bigger the leap, the greater the chance of hitting some turbulence along the way. Rather than avoiding it, I want you to be prepared for it, so it is easier to transition through it.

As you're doing your inner work and reaching for your goals, you'll experience wonderful breakthroughs, generating positive momentum and feelings of having it all dialed in. It's so easy to think positive and feel optimistic when you are in this state. You're naturally feeling confident with a high-level belief in yourself. Things seem to be going well, and there is a tendency to believe that you are on the other side of any old negative patterns.

What I want you to remember is that you are a creator by your very nature and have a divine inner calling for expansion and growth. So, while you're enjoying this positive momentum, there will be a subtle, but progressive, awareness of new desires – new levels of success. Maybe you want to do something new in your business to take it to the next level. Perhaps going from $1 million to $5 million in revenue, or from $5 million to $25 million. You want to elevate yourself to your next level in some way, shape, or form.

While you're becoming aware of this goal for growth – your heart's desire – I know from working with hundreds of clients for well over a decade that you will encounter resistance, doubts, or even fears that are subtle in the beginning and cause you to push off your desire for a bit. Initially, there's not a lot of negative momentum; however, the desire you have for growth keeps coming up (and so do the corresponding negative feelings). You can try to ignore it or try to justify that delaying it makes sense, or you might decide to embrace it and begin the process of moving toward it, coming head-to-head with those old, limiting beliefs that contradict who you feel inspired to become. Ideally, you will be mindful enough to do your releasing and reprogramming exercises. However, even with years of experience doing your inner work, big leaps can be challenging, and this is where having an experienced coach and mentor is extremely valuable.

As your awareness of the desire gets stronger, the inner conflict also intensifies. It's not uncommon for clients to come to me in this "breakdown before the breakthrough" stage. They've set a big goal or have a strong desire that's been elusive because of their old conditioning that is incongruent with their desired achievement. They don't understand why these insecurities are creating such huge obstacles. My comment to them: "You don't see it now, but this is actually a really good thing. It means you're right on the edge of a breakthrough. You're on the threshold of what your heart desires. We just have to get through this rough patch."

The breakdown before the breakthrough is the perfect metaphor to explain this phenomenon. In so many cases, it literally feels like a breakdown. It seems like our life is breaking down in some way, but it is our opportunity to clean up the old subconscious stuff that does not match what we want to create. You must let it go; you cannot bring these incongruent beliefs to the next level; it is not a mental-emotional-vibrational match to what you want.

Another phenomenon that occurs is that, although you have done some of your inner work, and seemingly resolved an old issue, as you are reaching for a next level goal, you will find yourself bumping up against that same old issue again. This is incredibly common and can evoke a lot of self-doubt and discouragement. So, what is happening?

Remember that we only release what's at the surface level. Essentially, we only release what is necessary for us to up-level, then we focus our attention on where we are going since we no longer have the resistance, and the positive momentum carries us forward. We don't go deep into the recesses of childhood memories and look for additional trauma or limiting beliefs on the subject, nor should we. First of all, you can never get through every misaligned belief in your subconscious mind. Further, searching for things to fix has you focused on problems and keeps negative vibrations active.

> *You don't need to go looking for things in your subconscious to fix. As you move toward your goals, any incongruent beliefs that need to be released and reprogrammed will show up.*

I promise you: Anything that needs to be

released will present itself along your journey. When you worked through that stuff in the past, it was good work. It was effective, and you have evidence to prove that. But there's residue of that old conditioning in your subconscious mind that's been there all along. Even though it wasn't active in your consciousness, there are still some old negative beliefs and associations that contradict and conflict with your new level and goal. Once again, *you cannot take these old beliefs with you to your next level as they are not a vibrational match to who you aspire to be, what you aspire do, and what you want to have.* You're facing another layer of disempowering programming that you'll need to clean up, so that you can up-level yet again.

Even though these various tripping points are extremely common, and don't feel great while we are going through them, understand that this is a natural process when we are up leveling our mindset and therefore our life. The old stuff you still believe that conflicts with what you want must be cleaned up.

Where's Your Focus?

Gaining momentum is about seeing the positive evidence and manifestations of the inner work you're doing. You gain positive momentum by being in positive emotional states with beliefs that are congruent with your goals. What if you are using the "tools" and not gaining positive momentum? Unfortunately, I see a lot of people who think they're helping themselves by using "tools" to fix all of their shortcomings but, in the process, are overly focused on negative old issues, keeping those lower vibrations active for an excessive amount of time. I'm sure you can see this is hurting more than helping.

Be mindful that, while you work to achieve shifts and breakthroughs that come from releasing negative, limiting beliefs, **your predominant intention is to spend the majority of your time in a positive state**. Feeling joy, love, gratitude, or enthusiasm enables you to be a match to even more positive thoughts, feelings, and experiences. You want to attract more circumstances and events that match the positive vibrations that, in turn, create more experiences that bring with them more of those good emotional responses.

Once you have this momentum, you'll find you need to spend far less time on the clean-up work. Yes, the clean-up work will still be a very important part of your process; however, the focus is not on fixing. The focus is on the joy of creating. Your inner work is about being aware of when you are slipping into a low vibration and then being proactive about cleaning it up by releasing the negative emotional charge and reprogramming by asking, "How would I prefer to feel? What would I prefer to experience?" And then get yourself into that emotional state. Always reach for a better emotion than the one in which you may find yourself if you are not feeling good – even if that is simply a feeling of emotional relief.

If you're in a positive state, all is well. Keep enjoying the feeling and enjoying the actions you're taking. It's when you bump into an emotional trigger that you must do your inner work. It's not about dwelling on the problem nor trying to figure out when and why something happened. That is almost always irrelevant and brings positive momentum to a halt by getting you stuck in trying to figure something out that appears to have no answer. Most of our negatively charged beliefs are nonsensical anyway.

Trust that when you do your inner work, if there is a higher learning or a more divine meaning or ah-ha moment, it is going to occur when you're in a higher vibration. You must release the negative emotional charge in order to move into

Mastering the Creative Process

the higher vibration in which you'll be able to reach the higher wisdom.

Your moment-to-moment awareness is a critical piece in creating a life and business you love. We've covered that extensively. Now I want to take a little time to get into the fun stuff – consciously creating what you want.

I've been studying metaphysical concepts since I was a teenager. The good news is, you don't have to be a student of this work for as long as I have to benefit from the core principles that you can put into practice today. Just remember, *the subtle nuances of monitoring and adjusting your state are the key to creating what you want.* Another quick disclaimer before the big reveal... manifestation doesn't always happen on our timeline. If you are impatient (low vibrational emotion), then you are actually interfering with the process and out of alignment with what you want. So, make peace with the timing and remember that as long as you are in a high vibrational state, good things are happening for you.

While our minds have been trained to believe what we see, the laws of the universe work differently. Essentially, we "see" the manifestational evidence of our internal state. That includes our beliefs, expectations, and our mental-emotional-vibrational state. When you want to deliberately create something in your life, no matter what it is, you must be able to clearly see it in your mind and feel as though it is your reality right now.

That is what we do in hypnosis, which is one of the reasons why hypnosis can be so effective. However, you cannot simply do this exercise one time, then think, act, and feel the way you used to and expect to get what you want. We've covered this, but it bears repeating. To master your life, you must master your mind and utilize your emotions as your indicator of whether or not you are in alignment with what you want.

When you first begin this process of visualizing with positive emotion as though you have the thing you want (experience, material possession, circumstance, etc.), your mind will tend to pull you back to your current circumstances. You'll experience doubt, or you'll find yourself thinking, feeling, and reacting the old way. Use the ALIGN process to clean up your energy and reach for the state of **having** what you desire. Feel as though it is done. The more you do this, the easier it will be to maintain the positive state. After a while, you will begin to believe that you will have your desire. And when you **know** that it is going to happen – there is no doubt in your mind – the manifestation will follow.

Throughout this book, I have been encouraging you to identify what you want and imagine it with corresponding positive emotion. Your ability to consistently reroute your mind to what you want each and every day is one of the single most powerful processes you can implement in your life. Intentional visualization and/or self-hypnosis sessions are a way to supercharge your goal achievement. Later in this book, you will find an introduction to self-hypnosis, which will teach you some fundamental principles for more effectively programming your mind to believe, expect, and act in accordance with what you want to create.

For now, I want you to take a moment to visualize or imagine having one of your desires fully manifested in your life. Get comfortable, take several deep breaths, and playfully explore in your mind what you'll be experiencing when you have what you want. Notice that you are seeing (in your mind) the things around you through your own eyes as though you are living it. Notice how good you feel as you are appreciating your life and what you are experiencing. Be aware of any other sensory experiences that might occur naturally. What thoughts are you thinking as you observe this reality? Are you conversing with others? If so, notice what is being said. Allow it to feel so real that you are temporarily experiencing it as though it is happening right now. And when you feel a sense of completion on the exercise, gently reorient yourself to the present moment knowing that you create your future. Revisit this exercise each day. In the morning right after you wake up and at night before drifting off to sleep are two of the most powerful times to imprint on your subconscious mind. However, you can enjoy the benefits of this exercise any time of the day.

Highlights About "Gain Momentum"

- Even though you start to experience breakthroughs and ah-ha moments, you are going to continue to bump into some of your limiting beliefs.
- Be aware of the "new level, new devil" phenomenon that occurs when you reach for the next level.
- The "new and unknown" often activates old, unwanted patterns, so be mindful of not allowing yourself to get stuck in the negativity. Stop and do your inner work.
- As you gain momentum, you'll likely become aware of new desires. That is your divine inner calling for expansion.
- With awareness of the new desires, you may experience inner and outer conflict; sometimes

- we experience a breakdown before we breakthrough.
- Just when you think you've resolved an issue, you may find it pops up again because we only released what was needed at that time to up-level.
- Gaining momentum is about seeing the positive evidence and manifestations of the inner work you're doing.
- While clean-up will still be needed, put your focus on the joy of creating, not the need to fix everything you believe is wrong with you.

Whether you find yourself in the breakdown before the breakthrough, you don't have as much positive momentum as you'd like, or you simply are 100 percent committed to achieving your goals and creating a life and business you love… Business Mastery Academy is loaded with resources that can truly help you break through. I invite you to take advantage of your free month at: www.acintl.us

Gain Momentum

Chapter Five
Nexus Point

We're now getting to the end of the ALIGN process: nexus point. The nexus point is the point at which we are mentally, emotionally, vibrationally congruent with our hearts' desires. We're in a natural state of positivity and aligned with our higher self.

That said, true alignment is not a state that is permanent – forever more. As with all of our emotions and dispositions, it fluctuates. You may have moments of being in true energetic alignment and moments when those old limiting beliefs lower you vibrationally. However, what we're ultimately reaching for is more consistent alignment that becomes our dominate point of vibrational attraction. When you're predominantly in alignment, you feel confident, feel a sense of meaning and purpose in your life. Your actions tend to be inspired. Of course, taking the inspired and higher vibrational actions are much more enjoyable and productive. In turn, results tend to be exponentially better than when you find yourself pushing through resistance and grinding through the day, forcing productive output.

Alignment is your state in any given moment in which you are congruent with yourself, your values, your actions. Energetic alignment is a very robust term. I generally use the word "alignment" to refer to that inner state of congruence. This concept can be a bit confusing to someone who's in a novice stage of this work. Perhaps, you had some confusion at the start of this book. Let me clarify: **Alignment is a state of being.** It's the mental and emotional state of allowing yourself to be a vibrational match to your heart's desires. You know you are in a state of alignment by the way you feel. Alignment feels natural, right, and good.

There will be areas in your life in which you have greater alignment. Things just seem easier. It may happen in your relationships or with your health. It's not uncommon for people to have, what I like to call, a "sticky" issue – one of the challenges with which they wrestle for a long time. You can enjoy success in many areas of your life, but despite your best intentions, there's that one issue that trips you up and has a lot of negative emotional charge.

At this point in the ALIGN process, you'll be able to more effectively work through any of those difficult issues. Armed with greater awareness, you can see there are a lot of incongruences in your subconscious mind with respect to that old sticky issue. There's misalignment between your existing beliefs and expectations and your desire. As you focus on this one area, you'll need to actively use the methods described in this book to clean up your energy on the subject and achieve alignment with your goals.

Attitude of Gratitude

In the process of creating a life and business you love, it's highly advantageous for you to be consistently reaching for the feeling of appreciation. You've probably heard about the benefit of practicing gratitude and perhaps wondered why it works. Authentic feelings of gratitude – not just going through the motions but being in a state of gratitude – carry a very high vibrational frequency. This high vibration essentially enables you to be in a state of non-resistance. This is a state in which you are not activating your triggers, limiting beliefs, and negative emotional charges on your unresolved issues.

When you are in the state of gratitude and allow it to be your dominant vibration for longer periods of time, you'll more consistently have positive experiences. Obviously, you will not always be in super high emotional vibrational states, but even softer, yet still positive, states – like a sense of peace or relaxation are highly beneficial. The key is that when you are in a positive vibrational state, you are in alignment with your true self. You are more of your authentic self in that state than when you're triggered and operating with limiting beliefs.

So, if you're examining the stickier areas of your life (those things you strongly want to change), you'll notice that it's easier to do your inner work on that subject from a relaxed state. I see many people who wait until they're highly negatively emotionally triggered to try to address the issue. I assure you, it is so much easier to release on an old limiting belief when you do not have strong negative emotions.

> *It's always more efficient to reprogram when you have a sense of peace and relaxation.*

This may seem like a contradiction since I want you to predominantly be in a positive state, so why would I suggest you work through your sticky issue after getting yourself into a positive state like gratitude? "Shouldn't I just stay focused on the positive?" The caveat is: If life is going great and you are feeling positive, don't go looking for things to fix as though you are broken and need to attend to everything you dislike about yourself. However, if you have an unfulfilled desire that is triggering negative emotions, your objective is to soften up your negative energy by reaching for a feeling of relief, so it is easier to work through your limiting beliefs. If you can release enough negative energy to get into a more positive state (sometimes you need to get off the subject completely for a while), then address your challenge from a state like inner peace or gratitude, it will be easier to shift the old negative associations with your challenging issue.

The state of gratitude is also one of the most effective states for programming your mind to achieve your goals and create what you want. So, as we are discussing the nexus point stage in the ALIGN process, it is essential to focus on the power of your mind and how to use it properly to create everything you desire for your life.

When I was going through my hypnotherapy training, the founder of the Hypnosis Motivation Institute explained you would never want to go to a therapist who's messed up themselves. While not his exact words, the essence is that you don't go to a dysfunctional person to work on reprogramming your mind. When you want to create new empowering mental programs with respect to that area that in the past was an issue, the same principle applies. How can you work on creating new empowering mental and emotional programs when you are highly triggered and feeling extremely negative? You can't expect yourself to reach any sort of high vibrational thoughts if you're mired in a negative emotional vibrational state. Therefore, we begin by releasing negative emotion first, then transition to reprogramming. Releasing the negative emotional charge allows us to move up into a more neutral state. From there, we can raise ourselves up into higher vibrational emotions by practicing visualization and imagining ourselves with the new beliefs and behaviors we want to program into our subconscious mind.

Vibration First, Manifestation Second

As we're on this journey, we tend to notice a lot of our superficial goals and desires lose their original allure. However, that doesn't necessarily mean they go away completely. It means that we're beginning to notice aspirations to be in alignment more of the time, feeling more positive, enjoying more moments of fulfillment, and having more meaningful experiences in our lives and businesses.

You may have heard the cliché: "Happiness doesn't follow success; success follows happiness." This refers to the energy principle that we covered in the beginning. You can only create that which is a vibrational match. If you are trying to create a successful, thriving business to live happily ever after, but you're miserable along that journey, guess what? You will be miserable when you achieve the success.

> *There's no "happily ever after" if there's no happiness along the way!*

If you're doing your inner work, and consistently feeling more happiness and harmony, you'll naturally feel more confident and empowered and be the vibrational match you need to be to enjoy success. Life will feel good. This is the transformational experience I want you to have.

Transformation is going from a lower vibrational state into a higher one. This is the process of transmutation – the state of being changed into another form. Energy cannot be created or destroyed. It can only change. You are essentially becoming an alchemist, but instead of turning lead into gold, you're turning your vibrational state from negative to positive. And I believe that's every bit as valuable as the lead/gold analogy!

Those old negative frequencies can transmute, and you become empowered to progressively shift that energy to create something wonderful, beautiful, and high vibrational. Isn't that what success is? Stop and think about what the vibrational essence of fulfillment is. Notice how high its vibration is. As you're on your journey, progressively reach for feeling more of this essence – the vibration of what you want to experience.

Applying the Laws

This is very practical and pragmatic. Notice that I'm not telling you to only sit, meditate, visualize, and wait hoping that what you want will somehow miraculously manifest in your life. We know the universe operates according to very specific laws. The law of gravity applies to everyone regardless of whether or not they believe it. The energetic laws apply to all of us as well.

When you have a desire, there will be a logical sequence of events that will occur according to laws to become a physical manifestation in your life. Sometimes you'll take inspired actions that lead to the outcome. Other times, it may seem that opportunities arrive at your doorstep and in your life. Maybe you meet the person who's perfect to help you with the next step on your journey to achieve your desired outcome. I assure you, 99 percent of the time, it is coming through what appears to be a very practical source… because that is how the universe operates. When you recognize that you are influencing those inspirations and circumstances that are leading you to the next logical step, then you'll understand the importance of your vibrational point of attraction and your predominant mindset.

Remember: Be mindful throughout the day about your emotional state. "This vibration I'm in right now… is this something I want to create more of?" If the answer is no, you must clean up your vibration, releasing the negative energy, and reach for a better emotional state. Of course, if the answer is yes, keep thriving. You'll notice that **when you are in alignment with your goals, you'll feel compelled to take action**.

You may have heard a lot of people say, "This law of attraction thing just doesn't work for me." Or "I should have achieved my goal by now." You may have been guilty of that comment (or thought) as well. Only when there's true honesty about the vibrational state you're in does the law of attraction "work." Let's face it. The law always "works." Whether or not the outcome is positive or negative depends on your own vibrational state!

Highlights About "Nexus Point"

- True alignment – the nexus point – is never permanent. Although you'll have fluctuations, reach for more consistent alignment and positive vibrational attraction.
- Authentic gratitude carries a very high vibration.
- Do not try to reprogram your mind when you are negatively emotionally charged. It's much, much easier to do this work from a state of peace and relaxation.
- You can't expect yourself to be able to reach any sort of alignment in your life if you're mired in a negative vibrational state.
- There's no "happily ever after" if there's no happiness along the way!
- Energy cannot be created nor destroyed. It can only change.
- When you have a desire, there will be a logical sequence of events that will occur according to universal laws to become a physical manifestation in your life.

Throughout this book I have introduced you to a lot of concepts that take time to truly learn and master. When I created the Academy, I took my years' worth of experience in these areas and put it into a large digital library of audios and videos to help you shortcut your learning curve and more effectively reprogram your mind to create the success your heart desires. I sincerely hope you will take advantage of the resources available to you. Your desire is a divine inner calling, and you can create a life and business you love!

www.acintl.us

Chapter Six
What to Do Now!

First of all, if you're reading this far into the book, I want to congratulate you. My publisher told me that most people who buy books never read past the first third! This tells me you are serious about achieving energetic alignment with your goals – about creating a life and business that you truly love. I applaud and support your commitment. There are two paths you can take moving forward. First, you can begin to put the principles, strategies, and exercises I've shared to use. I know they can and will help you. Second, you can speed up your progress, and perhaps go deeper than you ever thought possible, by working with me directly.

Throughout this book, I've encouraged you to practice the ALIGN process. While some people can easily learn from reading, others do better learning in other ways. In order to better assist your learning process, I highly recommend you utilize your free month of Business Mastery Academy. Inside the Academy are videos and audios to guide you through the processes and help you shift any old programming that does not support your success. You can start your free month at: www.acintl.us

Of course, I also work with a small number of private clients, and if you would like to explore whether working together is your aligned next step, you can schedule a confidential consultation at www.aliciacramer.com

My greatest desire is that you will apply the ALIGN process, and it will have a profound positive impact on your life. It has been transformational for me, and for my clients, and I know it can be for you as well.

Remember: You are a creator, and desire is a divine thing. You are not your past; you are not your current results; you are not your title nor your material possessions. You are so much more. You are a beautiful being who is full of potential, and you have your own unique goals and desires that when pursued from a state of alignment will create an amazing, fulfilling life and be a blessing to those whose lives you touch!

Bonus Chapter

Introduction to the Emotional Vibrational Scale

This is a short introduction to the emotional vibrational scale. I say "short" because there is a huge body of research work that supports this.

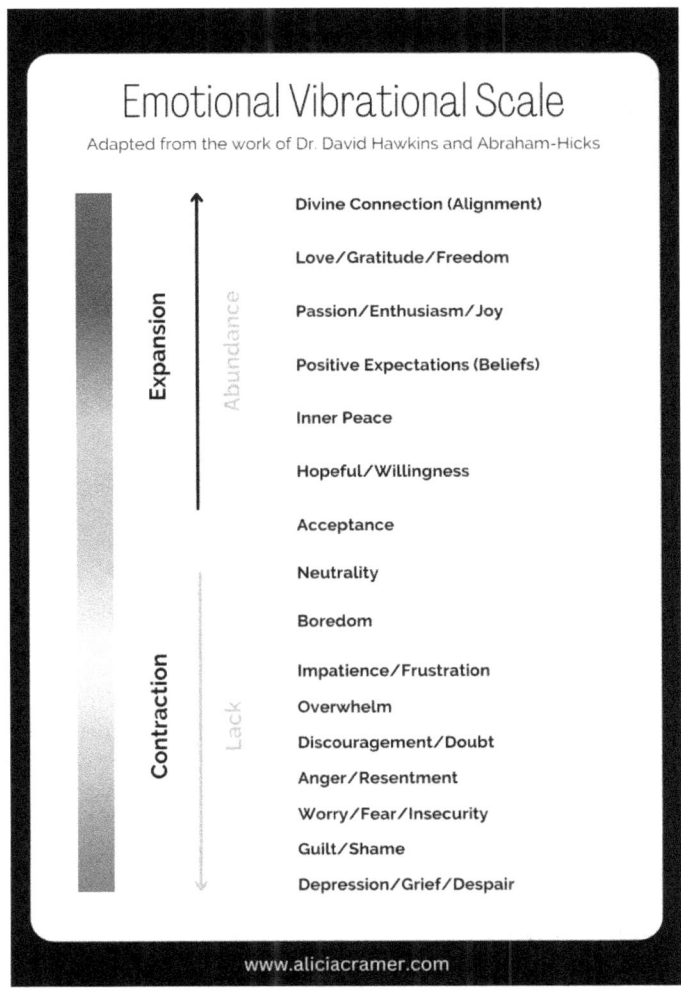

Introduction to the Emotional Vibrational Scale

Throughout the book, I've taught you that you must be aware of your current emotional vibrational state in order to change your circumstances and create the life you want. There are many different renditions of this graphic depiction. This specific one is my perspective based on years of experience.

Looking at the image, notice the emotional vibrational spectrum. Your awareness of where you are emotionally allows you to deliberately change it. We all feel a range of emotions. Fundamentally, you know how sadness or disappointment physically feels – heavy or constricted and contracted. There is an actual sensation that's a physical interpretation of the energy. Contrast that with the higher vibrational emotions, like love or joy. They feel lighter and more expansive. You feel the energy differently; you don't need any sort of sixth sense. It's already part of you as a human being.

Old triggers lead to feelings within the lower end of the scale. As you set goals and bump into your negative triggers, use the ALIGN process to shift the way you feel and retrain your mind to believe and expect what you would prefer. When you're feeling negative emotions, you might hear advice like "step out of your comfort zone" or "confront your fear." While a little of this is needed at times, typically this approach ends up negatively reinforcing the old pattern, so it usually doesn't work. A much more effective approach is to release and reprogram, so the actions you take are originating from a more empowering mindset and vibrational point of attraction.

Remember: everything is energy, including your thoughts and emotions. Emotions range from low to high frequency waves. When you're aware of where you are on the scale, you can reach for a higher emotion that is within range. It's important to keep in mind that you cannot make a large vibrational leap. For example, you cannot move from fear to love or gratitude in one step. It will not be sustainable. The shifts must be progressive in order to maintain a higher state. You can only take the logical next step. In many cases, what you are reaching for is a thought/emotion combination that creates a sense of relief. Remember my staircase analogy from earlier in the book. It's one step at a time, never a single leap to the top. For instance, you can go from sadness to anger. Then from anger to a neutral feeling. And from there you can reach for still higher vibrational emotions. Keep in mind, progressive doesn't necessarily mean slow. You can sprint up the emotional scale, just like you can sprint up a staircase. But you are still doing it in a logical sequence.

As an example, when someone is really locked into a low vibration and mired in a negative state, if you try to talk them out of it, it generally fails because it's working in contradictory fashion to the way the universe and law of vibration work. Rather, the better approach is to try to soften their negative emotion – a.k.a., taking one step – and gently help them improve more gradually. We're talking about making progressive improvements and getting some relief from intense negative emotion rather than attempting to jump right to pure positivity. Look at the chart again. While anger is a low vibrational state, it is a better one than the three that fall below it. It also carries more energy than you might feel when you are depressed or in a state of despair. Moving up the chart changes the wavelength of energy that we experience as negative to positive.

Some people can get stuck in a loop making progress up the vibrational chart only to have a triggering event send them downward again. Often, that's caused by a strong emotional charge linked to limiting beliefs, negative memories, and disempowering patterns. The ALIGN process helps to disassociate the negative emotion from the belief or memory so that you can more objectively think of the event or circumstance without the intense emotion. That will enable you to create new improved associations and break the negative cycle.

Many entrepreneurs struggle with impatience and frustration, and note that still falls at the bottom half of the chart within contraction and lack. If you find yourself here, your thoughts are not a vibrational match to the actions you need to take to create your desired outcome. If you're acting out of frustration, remember that like vibration attracts like vibration. The law of the universe indicates you'll only continue to attract thoughts, actions, and circumstances that give you more of the same. It is always contradictory to try to push through a negative emotional state rather than taking the time to do the inner work needed to clean it up.

Neutrality, as you can see on the graphic, is the baseline between contraction/expansion and lack/abundance. Beyond that, once you can reach a state of acceptance ("It is what it is; I am where I am"), you are on the threshold to move into the higher vibrational states, and you'll want to continue to move up and through them, step by step, taking the negative emotional charges off past memories and limiting beliefs and choosing more empowering thoughts and feelings.

Once you can maintain the higher vibrational states, you begin creating a life and business that feels good. And when you make these states your predominant vibrational states, keeping in mind that you'll go through fluctuations, your vibrational energy will attract more positive thoughts, actions, and circumstances.

When you are congruent in your heart and mind, and <u>believe</u> that you are creating your desired results, then you are in a state of alignment. From this state, the divine calling that's within you is energetically aligned and can manifest. This is when the magic happens in your life! Again, you'll fluctuate. I have yet to meet the person (and I doubt they exist) who is 100 percent in alignment all the time. However, even with fluctuations, when your predominant state is in the higher vibrational frequencies, you'll be creating a life and business you love and having a positive impact on others.

I want you to remember the simple but all-important question: "Is this emotional-vibrational state one I want to feel more of? To create more of? If not, how would I prefer to feel? What would I prefer to create?" You are creating your life
through your beliefs, expectations, and vibrational point of attraction. Your work is the inner work. Master your mind to master your life!

Introduction to the Emotional Vibrational Scale

Introduction to the Tools

Introduction to Emotional Freedom Techniques (EFT)

Emotional Freedom Techniques (EFT), also known as Tapping, is a powerful tool for releasing fear, stress, and other negative emotions that cause distress and block our success. It is also used for physical pain relief and other types of challenges. The most simplified description is that EFT is a combination of acupressure and psychology. The methodology was derived from Roger Callahan's technique, Thought Field Therapy that he discovered from his research into ancient Chinese medicine and their understanding of the human energy meridian system. Through a process of gentle tapping on a specific sequence of energy meridian points on the head, hand, and upper body, we are able to release stuck energy associated with emotionally charged memories and beliefs.

Although I am not going to go deep into the background of EFT, or even the science behind it in this book, my intention is to offer a brief introduction to the technique and encourage you to either watch the training videos on EFT inside of your Academy member's area, at www.acintl.us or learn more from the founder of EFT, Gary Craig, at www.emofree.com. There are also many practitioners doing various forms of EFT who offer free videos online.

EFT is best learned visually and audibly which I why I am only addressing it at a high level. EFT has been one of the most impactful tools for me personally and I have continued to teach it to my clients since 2006.

Introduction to the Tools

Introduction to the Tools

Introduction to Self-Hypnosis

Self-hypnosis is another tool that I highly recommend. I will not be going deep into the topic of self-hypnosis in this book; for more on the subject, you can read my book *Hypnosis for Success*. There is a digital version of it inside of the Academy. For now, I will focus on a brief overview of self-hypnosis and how to begin putting it into practice to help you program your mind to successfully achieve your goals.

Excerpt from *Hypnosis for Success*:

> Self-hypnosis often takes place unconsciously through self-talk and environmental choices. Effective (positive) intentional self-hypnosis, however, requires repeated effort and practice. It must be remembered that hypnosis is a highly complicated procedure and learning to hypnotize one's own self may not be as easy as it appears to be. Self-hypnosis is not sleep. When practicing self-hypnosis you should be fully aware of what you are doing. This calls for a great deal of clarity, focus, and self-control.
>
> Self-hypnosis can be learned successfully by listening to guided hypnosis audios, practicing the correct methods and procedures to induce the proper state, and/or training under a qualified hypnosis practitioner. When learning how to enter into a focused relaxed state, repetition and a positive attitude are essential. With repetition, you are training your mind to enter the state more quickly and effectively with greater ease and mental discipline.

Many people have adopted self-hypnosis methods to initiate positive changes and improvements in their lives. But it is important to warn here again that self-hypnosis can be unsafe if appropriate safety measures are not taken. Whenever you are putting suggestions into your mind, you want them to be empowering. It is best advised that you do not attempt self-hypnosis if you feel emotionally unstable.

How To Do Self-Hypnosis

Provided you are in a healthy mental and emotional state, chose a quiet comfortable location for your self-hypnosis sessions. You can sit in a comfortable chair or recliner or lie down.

Note: If you are prone to falling asleep easily, it is more advisable to sit upright in a chair.

Before starting, set a positive intention for your session. Establish your goal/desired outcome. Verbalize what you want to visualize yourself achieving and positive suggestions/affirmations.

Ensure there will be no distractions. Settle into a comfortable position. Now choose a point above eye level on the ceiling or wall and focus your attention on that spot. As you continue to focus your gaze, you will feel your breathing deepen. This is excellent; now become aware of each breath as you continue to focus on your spot. It is normal to feel as though your vision blurs and your eye lids begin to feel heavy. After only a couple of minutes, you will find it is much more comfortable to close your eyes. At this point, go ahead and close your eyes.

Next, you will want to create a deeper level of concentration and focus. With your eyes closed, imagine there is a mental screen or projector about where your spot was. Now visualize or imagine you see the number 10. As you count all the way down to 0, visualize or imagine each number. You can go deeper into this state by repeating this process three times.

Now you are set up for your objective. If your goal, for instance, is to enjoy exercise you would visualize or imagine yourself exercising and feeling great. Actually, feel the positive emotion as you create the imagery in your mind. If you are including affirmations, make sure they are positive and in the present tense. For example: "I love the way exercise makes me look and feel. I feel motivated and I feel great."

At the conclusion of your self-hypnosis session, you will count yourself out from 0 up to 5, with each count suggesting you are becoming more alert, energized, and feeling great. Use wording that feels good to you. At the count of 5, open your eyes, give yourself a couple of minutes to reorient yourself. You have just completed your self-hypnosis session!

Remember, this is a very simplistic introduction. If you want to take your understanding to a deeper level, there is an introduction to self-hypnosis training video series inside of Business Mastery Academy.

Energetic Alignment

Resources:

Throughout this book I referenced various modalities. While there are a lot of resources for each readily available online, here are some of my recommendations for more information on each:

ALIGN Process Trainings and Tools: https://www.acintl.us

Hypnosis Motivation Institute (HMI): https://hypnosis.edu

Emotional Freedom Techniques (EFT Official): https://www.emofree.com

Release Technique (Introduction to Releasing Processes): https://www.releasetechnique.com

Abraham-Hicks: https://www.abraham-hicks.com

Metaphysical Science: https://universityofsedona.com

Quantum Touch: https://quantumtouch.com

Neuroscience Research: https://neurosciencenews.com

Quantum Science Research: https://quantum-journal.org

Cover graphic is a visual representation of the human toroidal field. For more information I recommend:

HeartMath Institute: https://www.heartmath.org/research

Resonance Science Foundation: https://www.resonancescience.org/research-publications

For further advanced research on Human Energy Fields:

Shields D, Fuller A, Resnicoff M, Butcher HK, Frisch N. Human Energy Field: A Concept Analysis. J Holist Nurs. 2017 Dec;35(4):352-368. doi: 10.1177/0898010116678709. Epub 2016 Nov 23. PMID: 27881613. https://pubmed.ncbi.nlm.nih.gov/27881613

Leigh, G., Leigh, C., and Polonko, K. 2003, Differences in Human Energy Fields, Extension | University of Nevada, Reno, FS-03-68 https://extension.unr.edu/publication.aspx?PubID=4714

Purnell MC, Butawan MBA, Ramsey RD. Bio-field array: a dielectrophoretic electromagnetic toroidal excitation to restore and maintain the golden ratio in human erythrocytes. Physiol Rep. 2018 Jun;6(11):e13722. doi: 10.14814/phy2.13722. Erratum in: Physiol Rep. 2019 Jul;7(14):e13795. PMID: 29890049; PMCID: PMC5995311. https://www.ncbi.nlm.nih.gov/pmc/articles/PMC5995311

The Global Coherence Initiative: Opportunities for scientific research and health promotion - Scientific Figure on ResearchGate. Available from: https://www.researchgate.net/figure/Torus-Field-of-Planet-Earth_fig1_286869493

Our Weak Nonlinear Electromagnetic Field (Nemf) that Rules Everything in the Body is Emotionally Sensitive - Scientific Figure on ResearchGate. Available from:

Resources

https://www.researchgate.net/figure/The-human-torus-shaped-NEMF_fig1_330217977

In addition to the above-mentioned resources, I also highly recommend learning and practicing meditation and breathwork which in and of themselves are extremely beneficial and can further enhance the various processes and concepts covered in this book.

Energetic Alignment

About the Author

By trade, Alicia Cramer is a certified hypnotherapist, certified through the Hypnosis Motivation Institute, a nationally accredited college of hypnotherapy. She is also trained in many other modalities, including Emotional Freedom Techniques (EFT), having received advanced training through Gary Craig (the founder of EFT); Quantum Healing, Quantum Touch, and other less frequently used techniques. Alicia received her Master's Degree in Metaphysical Science from the University of Sedona, and attended Walden University for Psychology.

From a business perspective, Alicia's college education was in marketing. She has over ten years of business development consulting experience and truly understands the challenges that entrepreneurs face having spent time in the trenches with them.

Alicia's passion for the art and science of mindset reconditioning led to her EFT practice in 2006, which evolved into brick-and-mortar hypnotherapy practice in 2010. She transitioned from general hypnotherapy to business mindset coaching shortly after and now focus specifically on helping small business owners clean up their subconscious beliefs and behaviors to create businesses and lives they love.

To date, Alicia has worked with hundreds of private 1:1 clients and continues to offer digital programs, hypnosis audios and meditations, creating a wide reach to thousands of business owners around the world. Over the years, she has done numerous group trainings, helping coaches and other professionals across a variety of industries with her methods and approach, both from the mindset perspective and always with an eye on business growth.

Her extensive business background enables her to better understand the entrepreneurial mindset. Alicia has seen it from all angles and has "been there done that" as an entrepreneur who's also struggled and faced ups and downs.

Alicia Cramer's mission is to bring more consciousness into business by empowering highly driven entrepreneurs to get out of their own way, so they can create successful purposeful lives and businesses. She serves business owners in a variety of ways, including through her podcast, "The Mind of Business Success," her Business Mastery Academy, and 1:1 for a small number of private clients.

You can find information about Alicia's podcast, the Academy, digital programs for business owners, or private coaching services at **www.aliciacramer.com**

www.ingramcontent.com/pod-product-compliance
Lightning Source LLC
Chambersburg PA
CBHW050245220526
45465CB00002B/557